Northbook

Books by Frederick Morgan

*Seven Poems by Mallarmé—with images
    by Christopher Wilmarth* (1981)
Refractions (1981)
The River (1980)
Death Mother and Other Poems (1979)
The Tarot of Cornelius Agrippa (1978)
Poems of the Two Worlds (1977)
A Book of Change (1972)

Editor:

The Modern Image (1965)
The Hudson Review Anthology (1961)

Poems by

FREDERICK MORGAN

Northbook

UNIVERSITY OF ILLINOIS PRESS

Urbana Chicago London

*Publication of this work was supported in part by grants from
the National Endowment for the Arts and the Illinois Arts Council,
a state agency.*

Grateful acknowledgment is made to the following publications
in which the poems in this book were first published:

The Southern Review: "Northbook"

New England Review: "The Skulls," "Baby," "Tsalal,"
   "Metamorphosis I," "Metamorphosis II," "Exile," "Interiorly,"
   "Owl Head," "The Rishi," "Encounter," "Now that at last I must
   forego . . ."

The Hudson Review: "The Demonstration," "The Reflection,"
   "Visitor," "At the Hidden Springs," "The Diagrams"

The American Scholar: "I remember the sea when I was six . . . ,"
   "Alexander," "The Master," "The Gift"

Kayak: "Captain Blaze," "Omen," "Whore to Saint"

Sewanee Review: "Gawain," "Abiding"

The Yale Review: "Landscape in a Mirror," "From the Terrace"

American Pen: "Life"

Confrontation: "Do you seek a door?"

Harper's: "Castle Rock"

The Listener: "After"

The New Republic: "The Choice"

New York Arts Journal: "He couldn't believe . . ."

The New Yorker: "His Last Case"

Tar River Poetry: "The Wharf"

Virginia Quarterly Review: "The Murder"

"The River" was first published in December 1980 in a limited
   edition of 100 copies designed and printed by NADJA.

The author's translation of the poem by the Emperor Hadrian, which
   serves as epigraph to Section IV, was originally published in
   Michigan Quarterly Review.

LIBRARY OF CONGRESS CATALOGING IN PUBLICATION DATA

Morgan, Frederick, 1922–
   Northbook.

   I. Title.
PS3563.083N6   811'.54   81–14664
ISBN 0–252–00947–9 (cloth)   AACR2
ISBN 0–252–00948–7 (paper)

For Paula

"A simple dwelling, which shall be our own;
Where we will sit and talk of time and change,
As the world ebbs and flows, ourselves unchanged."

Contents

"And Paradise is between corruptibility and incorruptibility. . . ."

> Whence it seemed to me, that time is nothing else than protraction; but of what, I know not; and I marvel, if it be not of the mind itself?

ONE   *Northbook*

FOR MY MOTHER

The Tree

Rooted in doubt, you
        leaf out to the sun—
your foot is gnawed
        by an undying serpent.

Your hugeness harbors
        a billion selves
as you raise that dense ladder
        from world to world.

On your ultimate wrist
        the eagle perches,
rememberer, while
        the three veiled fates

water your roots
        from the well of conscience
as the still-to-be-wombed
        clutch darkly your boughs.

Odin

You tore out your own right eye, father,
not because it offended you
but to gain what you thought would be ultimate knowledge
from the person who sits at the roots of the world.
That lost eye shines through clear well-water

but in exchange you've found your double,
a second head to parley with
in time's retentive mirror,
a wisdom both your own and other
to instruct you in the perils of yourself.

And so, lavish of illusion, you hatch your plots
as though to delay the closure of the world—
aware the while that when the great show's over
(since gods have homes only where there's no knowledge)
you yourself can do no more than die.

Odin's Song

In pain I hung
on the wind-rocked tree
nine days, nine nights
while autumn deepened,
pierced by the spear
and given to Odin
myself to myself
as the cold came on

None gave me succor
of meat or drink
when I saw deep down
in the second world
black runes of magic,
ghost-engirdled,
clutched them up to me
and fell back screaming

Now your bodies are
forfeit to me
to be stabbed with the spear
and hanged on the Tree
nor shall I spare you
flesh-wrenching pain
poor children who seek
the knowledge that's mine

Heimdall

You are white clean through:
shadows pain you.
You can pinpoint the flea
at a hundred leagues.

Where the glad bridge ends
you keep watch at the brink
lest some polyp of darkness come
shambling up.

None who is stained
or spotted shall pass:
to the end of this time
we'll have clear demarcations

while you, bright god,
stand at one with your deeds. . . .
Who thinks to deny you
had best look within.

Freya

To the north, on bright days you may be seen
in your chariot drawn by white cats
moving across the fields, across the sky
blue-robed, your hair gold-streaming.

You do not acknowledge shadows or the grave:
of your thousand lovers you will save some few
according to your sole desire and choice
to live the aftertime with you.

To obtain the immortal necklace you gave over
your body to dwarfs, who used it loathsomely,
but you remained untouched by their disease—
as gold that's steeped in dung will still be gold.

Njord

Where sea meets land
        in shifting sunlight
are ripplings now, withdrawals. . . .

Sun on the rock
        through film of water:
glintings, sly dissuasions. . . .

God unconcerned
        half yields himself
in salt spray of inlets

and all's refined
        to subtle presence
where, absent, you reside.

Aegir

The gods drift down to drink your brew,
old alderman of the sea;
for weeks on end
they'll argue in your halls
unraveling their sleek expatiations.

Sensitive as they are
and keen in dialectic,
they see this tangled heap of ours—
the clenched dense world of meaning—
more finely than you'll ever know. . . .

But still your mumblings drown their clarities.

Ran

Severe lady,
your nets are out.

They are few whom I would bid you spare.

Jormungand

You rest unpleasantly
        on the ocean bottom
sluggish and muddy—
        hungry too, they say.

You go on a long way,
        all the way round, in fact.
When you caught up to your tail-tip
        you clutched it in your jaws:
from time to time you chew on it
        stupidly and sadly.

One has no conception
        of what your thoughts may be:
perhaps a clouded anger
        at knowing yourself alone,
or huge dim nostalgia
        for the time when all was one?

No matter. When you move
        come tidal waves above,
and one fine day you'll have your try
        at swallowing the world.

Thor

You have a big hammer
to solve all your problems with. . . .
Effective to a point, but not always apt.

When the time comes for making fine discriminations,
you head for the hills with that thing on your shoulder
looking for giants whose heads you can pound.

You kill the giants.
But more keep turning up
and anyway, the important problems seem to lie elsewhere—
like right back at home, in the gardens of the gods.

It's not easy to find your way through such tangles
and at times you admit you feel wasted. . . . Still,
you enjoy your meals, stay cheerful, and make ready for
 the end.

Frigg

Having already decided to salvage him
you took the shape of the hunted mountain goat
and led him on to your high castle:
when he passed through the glacier's door
and saw you smiling, he fell at once to his knees.

Later, of the various gifts you offered him
he chose the small blue flowers you held in your hand,
and you were well pleased, recognizing your man.
As long as they should bloom, so long would his own life
    flourish,
you promised—and dropped at his feet the leather bag
    of seed.

This was your gift of flax. . . . When the plants were mature
and the seed-heads had ripened to heaviness,
you came with your maidens down to his small field
and, greeting man and wife,
smilingly showed them how to pull up the flax plants
and steep them in water until their fibers loosened,
which—dried in the sun, then beaten with wooden mallets
and combed out strongly to separate the strands—
could be spun into thread for the weaving of fine linen.

He learned from you all that he needed and no more
and prospered in the unaging meadow
living the life he had once-for-all chosen
joyfully, through placid decades,
until the day when those first subtle blossoms
began at last to fade. . . .
Walking out then through a freshness of young plants
he searched the open sky.
"I'll see great Frigg once more before I die,"
he said to himself, "and thank her for my life."

Old and weathered
he set himself to climbing once again
while you in your silence awaited

behind the door of ice
that final meeting you had preordained.
"Enter, good friend, into my joy:
enter the home so cunningly prepared. . . ."
Words like these were spoken long ago
even before the man himself was planted—
and now he has arrived. . . . High goddess,
tell, if you will, the wonder.
To that cool lovely ecstasy of yours
does his mortality taste fresh and rare?

Tyr

It was because you trusted gods and men
as though all shared your large simplicity
that you put your hand into the foul beast's mouth

and lost it. And so there's an arm hereabouts
without a hand, while in the second world
a strong hand goes about on a shadowy arm
performing righteous deeds (for you sought to be righteous).

You never reflected, but paid the price of purity—
and now that a new word gathers in your head
remote and manifold, as from a mirror,
you find yourself unsure of what may threaten. . . .

Speak it out nonetheless! as the dark draws down.

Loki

Having said *no* more times than
the fates can count, you still
maintain that sinuous existence
bearing uneasily on ours.

A difficult love attaches you
to us, like strife,
from the instant the word is spoken
and you come dancing over the threshold
ready to serve or destroy—

for we value your touch of humor,
your willingness to see us through our scrapes,
but recognize at times behind the laughter
a huge shape sullenly cold,
grimly receding snakelike backward. . . .

You're a hater, it seems, after all—and wise,
for nothing is but merits hate
in all this stinking daily clutch
of what we call the human,

nothing but must be denied at last,
Denier, if we would be true—
nothing enduring but death in its changes
masked by the unstable glare—

while the world on its way to fire
trembles at the edge of meaning
as that which sustains it destroys it
in the frail moment's passing. . . .

Each day a new sun rises:
and you too are new each day,
ambiguous god whose flame
warming our ancient house
will burn it down in the end.

Loki's Song

Few may see
further forth
than when Odin
meets the Wolf:
so it is written
but I see plain
the great Tree shivering
in my flame

and you soiled creatures
who hindered me
charring to cinder
as I run free
across the earth's
old stunned domains. . . .
Pray as you will, I'll
scorch your bones

Balder

You were too beautiful to go on living,
too much a being of joy
for the present tense of the world:
you had to be put aside, so that
the process of things and meanings might be fulfilled.

And it was your brother, of course, who had to kill you,
sightlessly letting fly the misguided arrow
in sport, beguiled by the demon:
when he knew the truth, he retreated to the darkest
forest of the world, and starved himself to shadow.

The messenger was duly sent below
to negotiate your release
and "nature" wept for you—gods, beasts, and men.
But since there is always one who will not weep,
you must remain in bondage

mute in the clotted house
while here above, this age of iron
endures its last unravelings
awaiting the winter of betrayal
when the dead will rise with unpared nails,

the serpent lurch from undersea
and winds and wolves announce a day of flame
in which sweet flesh shall shrivel.
Ours, that approaching evil—
yours, this drugged suspension in the mirror-world. . . .

But after the blaze a newer day will dawn
cool and chaste, and the earth be green again
(or so it's promised) and from the resonant shade
of the great perished Tree a woman and man
walk out once more into the sun—and laugh

to find, in moist green grass
beneath a sky immaculate of pain,
the ancient golden chessmen of the gods.
Then you'll return, they say, in your loveliness,
leading your dark blind brother by the hand.

Ein begriffener Gott ist kein Gott.

T W O   *Monologues and Fables*

Captain Blaze

He told me to come around midnight, unobserved,
by the back way through the garden—so I parked the car
off the ocean side of the road, a little way down,
and walked twenty yards through the fog to his gray
    stone wall.
I saw no one else on foot, no cars, no lights.

That tall gate of white ash—all covered with pictures
he'd carved himself, of Pacific deities—
had been left unlatched as he'd promised: it made no sound
as I passed on through it and up the long flagstone path
between flower beds damply swept by billowing fog.

. . . You never knew him? I think no one knew him well,
and of course he had no friends: they were long since dead.
He was tall and stooped, very old but very strong,
leather-skinned, white-haired, clean-shaven, with
    yellowish eyes
(from atabrine maybe? He had sailed many years in
    the tropics)

and a fixed evil grin. But perhaps you've seen him in town,
moving slow and stately, leaning on a black knotted cane
and all the while wickedly smirking and smacking his lips?
Well, he wanted to consult me on a legal point, he said—
trusted me because I was of old New England stock

like himself, not some goddam dago, mick, or jew,
the new base breed that has sucked all the juice from
    our land
and rotted our northern strength with its vile weak ways
(those were his words)—it was something to do with
    his Will.
I admit I was curious: said I'd be over that night. . . .

There were steps to his kitchen porch. While I paused
    just outside,

23

trying to adjust, as it were, to the feel of the place,
I heard a low laugh sounding deep from within the dimness.
It wasn't repeated, but I'm certain I didn't mistake it—
so easy and strong, and full of a dark satisfaction.

I told myself not to be frightened, and went up the steps.
Once again a door gave: I entered and crossed to the kitchen,
a clean empty space dimly lit from its farther end.
"Captain Blaze!" I called out. "I'm here. I've kept to
   my promise."
No reply—so I moved softly on to where the light shone—

his dining room, I presumed. A single brass lamp
set high on a shelf near some books shed a feeble glow
over massed dark cupboards and chests and a huge oak table
from whose farther shore a seated figure glared. . . .
It was he—with a heart-shaking grin on his hideous face.

There were shadows all round, and it seemed as though
   something had moved—
which made me at first uncertain of what I was seeing,
of just what it was that confronted me there. Was he
   breathing?
Would he speak? Was there someone in hiding? It came to
   me then
he was dead, or caught up in a trance. I didn't dare
   touch him.

On the table before him were bottles—blue, amber, and
   purple
in various shapes, twelve in all. Could this be the secret?
Had he drunk himself strangely to death? No—they were
   bone dry.
What's more, from the cap of each one I found deftly
   suspended
a small piece of metal hung pendulumwise from a string.

I squinted and stared at them, wondering if here was a clue
to the vestige of movement I'd sensed a moment before
on entering the room: had these little ambiguous nuggets
been swinging, and winking, and ticking their messages up
to that old obscene horror who gloated and laughed in
    his chair?

Call me insane if you like. I don't care two straws
what word you finally hit on to help yourself through
your awareness of what may be deeper awareness in me—
for it's not very pleasant, I know, to come up against fear
of the kind that compels you to question your sense of
    yourself!

What had happened, and what was the point? Well may
    you ask,
but you won't get an answer from me: I can't comprehend
    it—
except in this sense I've kept of an evil communion
into which I blamelessly stumbled, or rather, was tricked.
—For I have this bad feeling I'm caught now, with lots worse
    to come!

You know all the rest. He was dead, they took him away,
and vandals (they say) burned his house down the very
    next night.
Because of the corpse's condition, bloat-bellied and dry,
the coroner found he'd been dead at least forty-eight hours.
I mentioned to no one I'd taken his call that same morning.

The Murder

When I heard the screaming, I ran back through the woods—
about two hundred yards, I guess—to the clearing.
I was tired—please understand—and somewhat confused,
having no idea what so suddenly could have gone wrong
with my father, whom I'd left five minutes before
standing, smoking his cigar, by the moonlit pond.
You see, I recognized the screams as his. . . .

I ran in a daze down the tree-shadowed path
and reaching the open space, stumbled and fell.
The moon was close to full. I'll never forget
how scrambling back to my feet I felt I was caught
in a trap of stillness and light. There were no more cries
and nothing in sight, as it seemed, except moonlit grass
and the glint of moon on the pond
and back in the elm tree's shade something darker than
    shadow.

I ran over. It was my father. His head had been smashed
and the poured-out blood and brains were soaking the soil.
God! I was numb at first
but then looking down at the corpse felt a rush of hate
so intense, it was almost as if I had killed him myself.
I felt the pain, too—but my hatred burned like a fever,
as though the whole vileness were due to him alone.

How long I stood there stunned I can't rightly tell—
maybe two minutes, maybe ten—and then I remembered
something else I'd seen from the corner of my eye
but paid no heed to at first in my trouble: a blur
almost too vague to be noticed . . . . The memory came
    clear.—
It was something gray as a rat, but larger and shapeless,
huddled off on the grass at the edge of the border of trees.

So I turned to it. Nothing! Gone. . . . Had I only imagined it?
I tell you I hadn't. It was something outside of myself

that came here from nowhere I know when my father was
   killed.
There is no more that anyone can say without going insane!
I was walking back home, as I've told you, when it all
   happened,
walking back home looking forward to my bed,
when a person or thing from far off came down to that
   clearing
and crushed my old father's skull by the light of the moon—
something I never never could have done
although I'll grant I hated the man like death.

His Last Case

—for Howard Moss

To solve the recent brutal bombings
they summoned Inspector Nayland Smith
out of retirement. For twenty-five years
he had been cultivating roses in an out-of-the-way shire,
leaving his old exploits to be whispered into myth

by those who remembered the poisoned earrings
of the Duchess of Devonshire, or those peculiar cakes
into which a royal personage's evil Afghan chef
had mixed mind-destroying drugs. "Smith, for all of
  our sakes
you must return to duty," the telegram read,

and the old man obeyed. Back in his dark office,
in a closet to which he alone had kept the key,
he found his black trunk full of multiple disguises
which he donned one after the other, cannily,
as he worked his patient way into the terrorist cells

like a subtle illness. He was gun-runner one week,
crooked financier the next, renegade priest the third,
infiltrating craftily the innermost councils
of the People's Select Committee for the Glorious Revolution
until he had identified each hidden enemy.

A year passed. The stage was set—
the ringleaders converging on a mansion in Belgravia
which Smith had wired in secret. Across the way
he watched sardonically from a shaded window,
waiting till his dozen fish had swum into his net.

It had just stopped raining. The cool quiet street
glistened with moisture as a cab whirled by
and two yellow-slickered children moved with hurrying feet
down the deserted pavement. They laughed in lilting tones
and Smith, for one moment, felt betrayed and alone. . . .

It was time. He gave the signal. "Show no mercy," he said,
"for the killers have shown none. . . ." His men took heed,
and when their work was finished, the Committee was
    defunct.
Remained only the obliteration of each treacherous cell,
the gathering in of accomplices and packing them off to jail,

and another brilliant victory was proclaimed by the press!
Smith received distinguished honors from a grateful Crown
and went back into retirement at the height of his renown—
but is said to have confided to one or two close friends
that he'll not return to duty when the bombing next begins.

"He couldn't believe . . ."

He couldn't believe it was there all along,
the life he demanded so angrily.
He called it, as he went on, by various names,
each—by choice—of a thing unattainable.

Taking no stock in imagined joys
he would keep up the search till he blacked out at last
in a death which he knew was the end of it all
and the end of him. Still, he felt uncertain.

His friend was at hand, but she wasn't enough
to assuage the bitterness of his need,
for his conscience commanded that life prove itself
before he concede the least show of acceptance—

and so, when she died, he felt all at once
the pain of losing what was never possessed
and a strangeness, as though his life had been severed
from some ultimate richness forever displaced.

Something, he knew, had been ventured on him,
and because he could be no jot more than himself
(whatever the stakes) that venture was lost.
He sickened, feeling the lurch toward madness. . . .

Then reading one day of those "Isles of the Blest"
hidden (it was said) by frost and mist
from ignorant eyes, he vowed once again—
holding fast to this hard-surfaced world as he knew it

and scorning the solace of beautiful lies—
if a goal were not tangible, not to pursue it. . . .
Thus sworn, he felt himself smaller and stronger.
The road not taken was there no longer—

his life now justified his anger.

Castle Rock

—In memoriam Lillian Vissenga

We climbed to the very top that August day
while the others waited below
and time reached back one hundred years.

The immense stone forming the capital of the cone
was bare of soil except in crevices:
overhanging by several feet on every side
the huge earth mound on which it rested,
it had the look of being gravely poised
on its own center—a trifle insecure.
Would our small added weight set it tilting?

No matter—we climbed. Insinuating ourselves
lithely into fissures and over projecting knobs
we worked our way, ascending, around the sides
to the upper surface, a breezy platform
smooth as a tabletop and open to all four points.
Hawks wheeled and screamed from their colonies of nests
on one side of our pedestal,
while down below us little hares were playing
in the ashen furze that thatched the earthy mound
and antelope grazed, far off, on the gray plains.

I dreamed I was my grandfather recalling
the landscape of a lost America—
and took your hand. Hours passed. When we descended,
the sun, declining, bathed the far brown mountains
in a rich amber glow, and deepening shadows
shrouded our patient friends. . . . "It's the true end,"
you whispered musingly—and all was silent
as we resumed our memory of the present.

Gawain

—for Robert Fitzgerald

Strange, those lighted windows on
an axis running south to north—
their ironies precede us. Now
the night looms vacant like a church
as we walk its floor of hidden lakes
(two comrades in December's dying)
noting no gladder signs of life
than plantlets needing little light. . . .

Woman bound steadfast to the earth,
I have hung many shining thoughts on you
in trust you'll gain the realm prepared
for those who risk this winter journey—
while I, considerate of the year,
as fabulous beast with leafy horns
(delightful to think of, is it not?)
subdue my neck to the green chapel.

But first, our vision. . . . The radiant Child,
once wrapped in spectral blankets, who
holds out his piece of bread and butter
though earth be mortmained to the snow,
making us know by no word spoken
what the unshadowed life retains
that grants this weakling world no taste
of its lost elegance and pain—

since he, according to the legend,
long ago was pledged to our aid
he'll not return yet to his senders,
having once crossed to the animal side
(for which my breath shall ever praise him
though it be but a dunghill fume!)—
this Child of the strange heavens is
our child too, Lady, and no blame.

Before all else, I trust I'm human:
my head, which I must shortly lose,
signifying imperfect reason,
poor working model of high grace.
Remembrance never will replace it!
but let my painted portrait hang
obdurate in your private chamber
when you're restored to your domain.

The Skulls

Three human skulls had been tossed into an alley,
    a gritty back alley in Todentown. They were
    brownish-white, pitted. They whispered in the dawn.

"How shall we tell the living ones the truth—the truth
    we know so well? What is, today, the truth we know
    so well? How do we know the living ones will listen?

There is no heaven or hell, so we believe. There is no
    afterlife at all, so we and they believe. Yet here
    we are, whispering.

Are we whispering prose or verse? Things are pretty bad,
    we know, but they're going to get worse. Do the
    living ones feel it in their bones?

This is not an afterlife for real. But we've seen our
    bodies' shadows, passing by. And other shadows too
    at odd times: human beings (as they're called),
    dogs, cats, crocodiles, gorillas. . . .

We would like to tell the truth to everyone. We would
    like to tell them how they all must end. We would
    like to tell them how the world and all that's in it
    has to end—

maybe with a gasp or two, likely with a bad smell, the
    whole show slithering into rot. . . . That's all there
    is to tell,

and we'd like to shout it to the living ones and make them
    face it! But now and then, we must admit, things seem
    less clear, more complicated

because, you see, here we three are (whatever we are),
    whispering. . . . Yes, old bones hang on, it seems—
    what about old thoughts and dreams? Maybe they don't
    give over right away, or not completely—

maybe a mirror right about now would help us see the truth
more clearly: see ourselves as part of it, see
mirror-in-itself as part of it—

maybe a mirror is what we need to see ourselves as
skulls that see—

yes! how we wish someone would toss any old cracked
mirror back this way: back into this junky pitiful
poor excuse for an afterlife, where we don't have
anything left to do or say

except stare at one another in mild surmise, wondering
about truth and the holes that were our eyes:
wondering about that blessed deadly truth we're
desperate to proclaim

and must be a part of, are surely a part of—because here
we are, whispering."

Thou shalt descend into thy inner man, and
see if there be any traces of a soul there.

T H R E E   *Riddles and Evocations*

Life

Life takes hold of you sometimes,
makes you a speaking reed,
speaking in self's despite
words that could never have been foreknown as true.

Gleanings? Perspectives, rather,
opened to the moods of time
so that life's daily plainness
shifts and dissevers to the darkening view.

Then, moving on through days
weeks years of hazarded life
once more you speak as you can
words so unsparingly known they must be true.

Baby

The baby bit the snake in two
who came to tempt him in his cradle:
he would have swallowed, if he were able,
mom and dad and the serpent too.

What child is this? Not you nor I,
surely, would be so grossly crude
even in swaddling clothes! Too proud
to strike, we hoard our bites and die.

A whitesnake soup is good for the brain—
unplugs the ears to the speech of birds—
but this starveling babe lisps into words
his venomed yearnings all in vain.

"I remember the sea when I was six . . ."

I remember the sea when I was six
and ran on wetted sands
that were speckled with shells and the blowholes of clams
bedded secretly down in black muck—

I remember the sun, fishy airs, rotting piers
that reached far out into turquoise waters,
and ladies in white who sprinkled light laughter
from under their parasols. . . .

Where was it, that beach whose hot sand I troweled
day after day into my red tin pail?
It's only in dreams now I sense it, unreal,
at the end of an inner road no longer traveled.

Alexander

Alexander cut the knot,
couldn't be bothered to untie it:
he wasn't good at solving riddles,
wouldn't even try it.

His adolescent blade addressed
the ancient hide and pierced clean through it.
Triumphantly he failed the test
and never even knew it.

Tsalal

The very rocks were novel in their mass,
color and stratification,
and the water had the consistency of gum arabic;
when the savages saw the carcass of our white beast
they fled to the uplands with harsh wailing cries.

Innocent of the meanings that were carved
grimly into their isle's black carapace
they killed us all except my double and me.
We had our vengeance later, when
the white estrangement leaked through southward
  curtains. . . .

It whistled, and the whistling drove them mad
so that their black teeth tore their own black flesh—
the while our great canoe,
poleward dividing feverish seas, attained
this emptiness past all conciliation.

"Do you seek a door?"

Do you seek a door?
> *A corridor*
down which these steps will pass no more

Do you seek a way?
> *A hideaway*
where none but the extinct may stay

What meaning does this leave you with?
A skull's meaning, who saves his breath

Do you seek a gate?
> *A runagate*
opening worlds outside my fate

After

The clouds were moving to the east
that day: I found you lovely
as though all pain were held in hands
that opened and released.

Later I walked outdoors at midnight
down the small-town streets
thinking of hair bleached white with age
and a lion starving in his cage.

Someone was playing the clarinet
softly, behind shutters
through which dull orange light spilled softly
down the gray house-side.

I thought of you between white sheets,
private and alone,
and wondered would I move in your dreams
at all, when I had gone.

Metamorphosis I

The waves were friendly (though cold)
like mirrors to which he surrendered his final sense
  of himself
in an act that was somehow too much for the simple land.
The sun made no comment, observing his getaway. . . .

Where would his mind take him next? He didn't quite know
but assumed an ancient fiefdom beneath the sea
where shedding again the soiled and aching pelt
he'd meet, on some greensward, his bright thousand wives.

Metamorphosis II

It was midnight, and cold. From the inn
a few steps behind me came blurred
half-smothered mumblings and clinkings.

I looked down the road. She had gone
but a moment before in her rage,
her hair a hard helmet of gold,

the goddess. She had vowed my destruction,
and what could I do but honor her
still, in her evil whore's guise—

I, who have seen her emerge
naked and suave from the wave
and felt the dense clench of her passion?

Exile

Ovid forlorn by the Black Sea,
old Ezra penned in his cage,
have nothing more to say to me
though the green man rage.

By Lac Léman the music stops.
I quail—but from afar
the voice of Basil still resounds:
"Solve et coagula."

The Wharf

Smells of oil and tar and fish
    drift from beneath the wharf
where easy water laps and lags
    in flickering shadow.

A place to brood and meditate
    (when you have time to kill)
on why the river's never the same
    and never the same this life.

It alters, it moves on and on—
    and yet that fishy stink
merges me in the one I was
    who still survives these changes.

They found a human skull one day
    down there in the dark water:
it's all the same to him, I thought,
    his changing is no matter.

Whore to Saint

Barefoot, the pensive whore
walked an Ionian shore.

Great waves that shieldlike shone
in brimmings of the long dayshine
freshened her gritty shins.

From far beyond Teos a fathomless wind sliced in,
breath of the alien god,

and a voice spoke: "Woman, the passageway is yours."
Eyes open now to remoteness of white sails,
she breathed her release from the ancient coil of wars. . . .

Yes—resurgent spirit shuns
the noonday blaze that crowns and stuns:
she worked once for all her sacred stunt
(of love that's emptied without stint)
at fall of dusk,
                    this sea-changed saint.

Interiorly

Interiorly
the space is opened
unto the god, unto the god they say

as when I dreamed
of my grandmother standing
in the quiet room at the foot of the stairs

who had risen to greet me
and one other
(the late sun glowing through the long French window)

and who was the other
I never knew
waking in my bed to the scent of verbena.

Owl Head

"What is the purpose of being alive?"
asked the old owl head.
"I'll have a heart attack and die,"
it sourly said,

"for if I cannot be the first
I'll not be at all—
better move off this worldly perch
before the fated fall."

The Master

When Han Kan was summoned
to the imperial capital
it was suggested he sit at the feet of
the illustrious senior court painter
to learn from him the refinements of the art.

"No, thank you," he replied,
"I shall apprentice myself to the stables."

And he installed himself and his brushes amid the dung and
    the flies,
and studied the horses—their bodies' keen alertness—
eye-sparkle of one, another's sensitive stance,
the way a third moved graceful in his bulk—

and painted at last the emperor's favorite,
the charger named "Nightshining White,"

whose likeness after centuries still dazzles.

Omen

A car with ten headless dead bodies in the back
rolled up the slopes of Mt. Cadillac
and launched itself creaking on the stunned August air—
the blood from its axles rained red and rare.

Night fell. The car jaunted black among the stars.
The bodies stretched and strutted and made prophecy
    of wars—
while the ten heads, muttering a lucid speech,
swam the chilly narrows of Frenchman's Reach.

The Rishi

The Vedas exist
from before creation,
pattern of God's mind:
the Bible came along later

as a kind of apology
by jealous grim Yahweh
so harsh to the Jews,
perhaps needing an excuse:

this personal god
just and austere
but infected with desire
must yet be obeyed

(so the Rishi taught)
until one sees through
to the void where he's joined
to his passionless ground.

Encounter

I met at noon the white-haired oldster, walking along
    easily—
loafing along, as he would say it, loafing along easily—
and we both stopped still. "This is a surprise," I said,
"I thought you were dead."

"And so I am," he answered laughing, "dead as anyone
    can be—
but still I like to wander past the crossroads now and then
where the solid earth I love is joined to the mindscape of
    a friend—"
he paused, and stroked his beard.

"You're kind," I said. "Never kind," he answered, "only
    true—and truth to tell,
you weren't very likely, but you've turned out pretty well—
a better friend than some who make the claim. So long!" He
    went his way,
his strong back vanishing through the trees.

"Now that at last I must forego . . ."

Now that at last I must forego
the ocean and its soundings
quietly, quietly
I'll travel only where it suits my fancy. . . .

As into blades of grass
moist-green at first dawning
or smudged soiled understones
of crumbled factories at the city's edge:

severe into root and rock
as into anguished love,
urging in dark clarity
this voyage to an inner day that brightens.

Soul, little wandering friend,
companion and guest of the body,
to what regions now are you drifting—
naked and pale and constrained
with no hint of the old repartee!

FOUR

Ten Dream Poems

The Choice

A clear sky may tell it wrong
when its warming light crosses
eyes and arms of a woman you have loved
and a blue pitcher standing on the window table.

All is bright, and must rejoice
in the sea-light gleaming across to the foothills
as wordless the barley sings outside,
"Think now of November."

Pinned by the exacting sun, the heart
grows its second skin
but always fire has a last word
and speaks it out, no matter—

speaks it out to the troubled ghost
rising at night from a wakeful page
who moves in the shadows of the woman's room
like a man of ash and water.

The ocean girdles this sliding earth
as the hopeful lover chooses,
not knowing the face that will be revealed
to a new sun shining through. . . .

The woman has a tranquil look
but the room seems gathering in a tear
as he sits in his studious chair all night
reading the breathing book.

Abiding

"Abiding in the spirit of loving-kindness"
(at least for a time) I made myself a list
while Tristram's eyes glared savagely from
the oldest axioms in the book.

I noted rain that fell like judgment
on forgotten gardens at sea's edge
where, all unversed in modern pretexts,
Tristram rehearsed the doom of swords.

Nor was his love matter for reflection,
but a law by which his life was shaped
to daily circumstance. . . . I noted
how chance gains power over such "mistakes,"

and how philosophy as we have known it
can be but a blinded eye at best
when winter's ice breaks in derision
and a few strong weeds raise their sightless heads.

The Demonstration

It seemed to be a monk, plausibly disguised
in the tried-and-true attitude of the Dying Gladiator,
who was seeking to propound to me some "ultimate"
  question. . . .

But while I watched, the scene changed again
in this cosmologic handsome picture-show
to a plain country kitchen where a woman's hands
were shaping white flour into pillows of bread
as a mouse walked tiptoe on the faded ceiling.

It cannot be, then, the lie you lie expecting
as a footbridge of remarkable length from hell
that becomes the subject of the demonstration

these days (these nights): no, not by any means,
you cannot play dead in the unspeakable limbo
(spiritual tremors marking out the soul's passage)—

I am not dead but have lain down to rest
in my silent sleepy bunk-room along about twilight:
the outer wall is eight foot thick,
and down on the beach white sand has drifted
negligently into elegant dunes,

and I work a slick witchcraft that joins to beauty
as we suddenly set sail on the antarctic sea
(it is plenty light enough) where the wind sends curling
little pallid waves like lazy whips
while at daybreak a curlew screams out my living word!

I'll not come back—do not wait upon the shore,
kind frivolous women from time's abyss,
do not yield to expectations of what nature may demand

but remember to the last those berries that bloom
purple and russet in your hinterland shades
with the thrush that speaks at nightfall, and
the wild Sileni in their caves beneath the mountains.

Landscape in a Mirror

Though we saw it all leaching, blowing away,
we stayed where we were, mutely unapt
for such masterly changes in strategy as
the savage trompe-l'oeil appeared to demand.

Male and female, more apparent than real,
we were leaving behind us areas of destruction
quite as though no more foundation were needed
for Emerson's diecast of man over nature.

The chosen tree falls, crashing to the flat land,
and a large signboard with the inscription "Humanity"
is raised in its place: the rituals are elaborate,
and manifold the objects of thinking and feeling,

but we've drifted away from the initial difference
who once could be called on as musical gods
to flaunt the panache of peace and fulfillment
on sober displays of an external world. . . .

Heartfelt deep love is what matters, they say,
but I feel as in dream a sort of amazement
remembering how lately the Lords of the Tomb
could find our poor earth-smells so random and shocking.

The Gift

By day she sat at the top of the house
where opposites of space and time
kept her for ever out of his reach.

How to remain what he was at that moment,
a stream flowing forward into the future?
Longing to worship some goddess of the dawn
he nonetheless knew what went on behind his back.

Reluctant movements behind the bleached curtains:
"I would kill you rather than let you touch me!"
Though the shadow realm lay open, he knew
(offering at the threshold his keepsake of wine)
he'd get but a portion, not the treasure.

And yet, her hand had once rested on his
in joyous neglect of clothing their dead!
Now, bare-breasted, she nursed a male child
as the dark tertium quid stood by like a shadow

muttering his toll of illusions. . . . No help—
no help for the cindery man of reasons
who, lucky but once, had received her as gift.

The Reflection

Among night-time tribes, in the night-time forest,
accusations of witchcraft are leveled against the women:
on the tenth night they learn to turn to jaguars and bats
and are harried to the sky where they enjoy celestial visions.

Out of my six wits with anxiety and grief
for the wanderer lost on my backward shore
I was recognized at once in Schadenland
by one who reached a paw out to pluck my shirt.
He led me to the central hut within a muddy clearing.

A skeleton dangled from the roof's overhang
who began to creak and clatter at my reticent approach.
It seemed he was distempered by the course of these events!
A huff of jungle night-breath proved his sudden
    ruination. . . .

I knocked at the hut door. My companion changing shape
was a gravid insect-thing who bumped the ground and
    whimpered—
a kind, I thought, to fill my ears at night with slippery eggs
that would crack and leak their venom. . . . Turning on the
    seductress
I spurned her frothy mandibles as the door inched
    gravely open.

Inside, in firelight, a huge black king
was carving men and women, most delicately, of wood.
They sprang to life unmindful of a ghost's imploring gaze
(it was Rimbaud's played-out doubleganger, dismal and
    disheveled,
assuming kill-joy attitudes behind the black left shoulder)

and walked out past me silently. A shadow sun was sinking
as I strained to see those faces: men, women, a few
    children—
persons I had known once on the day-shores of ocean—
moving to the darkening wood, comprehending nothing.

—Clothe me in jaguar skin, give me secret wings
to ride the difficult air of this sardonic vision
that enunciates a night-sky to a million aching tribes—
but do not ask me, like a luckier man, to propound:

for I reckon from what radiance my revenant has come
(as between eons of night, they say, flash ribbings
    of perception)
and how it will outlinger every timely shift of shape. . . .
Let the dark knowers range at large through moonless
    hemispheres
and chessmen wander blindly, ignorant of their squares!

Everything that breathes in the origin, is the origin.

At the Hidden Springs

The water-sounds flowed on reflexive
suggesting a new brief happiness
for the one who burned insane with rage
buffeted in darkness by living men.

The alternative, of course, was non-existence:
and what a grim gap he'd leave behind
thanks to that fabled strength of will—

huge cities leveled to the ground,
fists crashing down into misshapen faces!

I shut the doors of my mind to it all

and laying my hand across his mouth
told him I wished I could forget

(as though one might fall asleep at last
finding such difficulties of little substance)
this time of filth and treachery. . . .

Then we moved through a world of flowers and books,
the rage being overcome, as it seemed,
and he put on the wreaths of a pagan god
and blessed the past from which he had foundered.

From the Terrace

Lucidity of the unredeemed. . . .

His presence there below, at a table in the cafe,
wearing as always the pince-nez and bowler hat

distressed us so, one summer afternoon
(as though he were a revenant to be exorcised
from any but the subtlest meditation)

that you and I, becalmed in our own breathing,
dwindled to ghosts of self: when, standing clear,
I suddenly put on his skin like a fiery shirt,
feeling his bones at a great distance inside my chest,

and so ran down that sandy beach at Savanna-del-Mar
to where a beautiful white flag was flying
and a woman's breast rose humming like a beehive
gently from the substance of dreams—

and there resigned all hope of keeping back the dark
(when her hand gleamed white from beside the farthest
    cypress
beckoning now a night-sky crammed with stars)

until we two had passed beyond this imprecision
back to the terrace, back to moods of sleep

with our quitclaim to the unseen chain of selves.

Visitor

The visitor looked across the bright pond
where goldfish floated, belly up—
a young man, long and strangely lean
in this world of the shades of shadows.

Behind the great house the sun munched dust
while the children kept busy with their growling and
    playing—
perfect circles, of such nicety—
in that precinct of dire retrievals.

Would the feasts be infrequent, and of infinite bliss?
Such an ideal had all along existed
among noble deities and earthbound demons
as body dragged soul down, down into the mutable.

This dream would reveal no particular person
or place, the garden in which he reclined
being exiled, it seemed, from what purposeful roads
and crossing-places had been found exemplary—

yet "every nature with which heaven will be filled"
had unshrouded itself to that setting sun. . . .
Softly in the dusk a woman was singing.
A light wind kept waking him, as if into battle.

The Diagrams

The large rains had long since passed in thunder
when I became the subject of a threatening monument
in the old park, by the ocean's edge.

Dismal Sundays! In deliberate stages,
like a pharaoh advancing through the Underkingdom,
I evaded the snares of those excellent sermons

delivered by a mock-man with glittering teeth:
a mother, it seemed, had lost ten sons in battle
and even in dreams breathed their acrid scent.

This was a marvel. But all the while I thought
of you, Clarissima, eyes vivid as moons,
who hold in your depths a thousand melodies

which the fairest landscape may never accommodate:
has the Prince not stared through his diamond lens
all autumn, believing you incapable of folly?

Weighed down by winter now, the ponds are dozing
while five guileful lunatics (impersonating angels)
in worn leather jackets saunter beneath the smoke

of decadent December. . . . It's the last fastening
(not that any amount of luck will accomplish it),
the last fascination. . . . And farther down the coast

ten thousand wild geese fly in from the north
to the philosopher's cove, and ice begins to gleam
on flashy rivulets, and bacon fries in cottages,

and the women expose their cunts in the cement factory
to idle come-and-goers, to angels with blond wings,
though all afternoon one body is not present. . . .

The Image may divide, then, into ghost and lasting bronze,
in different centuries walking the same forest
to the ocean's margin, where an old park awaits—

but I, expectant of the dusk, outlinger these charades
in the moon-eyed progenitrix's hazardous kitchen
(among lightnings elusively aflicker after rain)

and watch a milky she-cat chew the old Book's random pages
as I offer at the hearthside of devious time
these diagrams, homes of the dead.

Nous nous réveillons tous au même
endroit du rêve. . . .

FIVE   *The River*

FOR PAULA

The River

1

A fresh June morning
    your dress flung across the chair-back
and birds awakening,
released from the book of night.

Here it is, the Day
    like none other from world's beginning
and all we have is in it:
I read you again and again.

2

The sun tells stories
    to the restless river
as the trees listen in.

The river is resistless—
but the trees recall the rain's
lisping insistent voice
urgent at the back of our minds

while the sun tells his stories
    (familiar, widely applauded)
to the river of every day.

3

Two bodies in the river,
yours and mine, moving,
a midday swim. The sun
is sultry and relaxed.

    Have I taken hold of your hand then?
    Is there such sweet ease between us?

It's as though the river sums it all
in our minds and its own.

4
Now you are holding a book:
intelligence there with passion
suviving the individual brain and hand—

and when you speak of it tellingly
as we walk beneath the trees
    a living ghost stirs
in the world where all our thoughts are trees and rivers.

5
Decisions of afternoon: as,
to swim once again in the river
before the day turns dark? or
to read from a book of adventure—
of the kind refused by the crowd?

Whichever, it will be private,
unhandled by the human
except as what is human
may also be river and sun.

6

As the sun dims we begin to think
    of evenings that may have passed by
in the world only the trees know.

Only they know it because
    it's a world deprived of vision
and metaphysical striving,

a voiceless world of dense fabrics.
    You and I holding hands
touch on one corner of it.

7
Sleeping, we boarded a boat
that went drifting through our heads
down dark reflective aisles of
summertime water.

The bitterns and Spanish moss:
a Carolina dream.
Uneasy voices called out, too,
beyond the vegetable islets.

Floating, we were hand in hand,
and when our bed returned
it was as though the book had opened
to our reflective eyes.

8

A voice spoke in the night
      while the stars moved slowly
within our dreaming heads.

Not in ancient thunder, not
in the still small voice of the Lord,
but with something like
the rain's persistent utterance. . . .

Insatiable rain!
      Our bodies clasped and clasped.
The weak stars winked out.

9

Morning. A river view
calls out to us obscurely:
you are your naked body, crossing
whitely the open room.

Sunlight tips the trees
as if to say, A beginning.
No more is to be said.

The book lies on the bedside table:
once, it contained the night.